Habits & Habitats
BIRDS OF PREY

John Andrews
Photographs from Ardea London

Introduction

Birds of prey are hunters – keen sighted, sharp-eared, swift in flight and deadly in attack. They are feared by many creatures, some of which spend their lives with one eye cocked to the sky, venturing into the open as little as possible and always ready to run for cover. Others – equally alert and agile – are able to fight back with teeth or sharp beaks, claws or talons, venom or stings. In spite of this, birds of prey seem to be able to find and kill food almost without effort and many have become so cunning and so strong that they can overpower animals far bigger than themselves.

They are instantly recognizable. When you see those needle-clawed toes and the downcurved beak, it is obvious that the soft plumaged and cuddly-looking owl perched motionless, apparently half asleep, slowly blinking its mild, round eyes, is just as much a killer as the massive, monkey-hunting harpy eagle with its horned crest, its fiercely glaring gaze, hunched shoulders and heavy, taloned feet.

Birds of prey may be found almost everywhere in the world – except in the permanently frozen lands of Antarctica. Some soar high in the thin, cold air over tall mountain peaks. Others fly swiftly between the spreading branches of hot tropical rain forests or hurtle, bullet-fast, into the flocks of feeding birds on a misty estuary. A few seek crouching birds or animals amid the snows of Greenland. There are those that capture bats as they leave their daytime roosts in the warm summer dusk, while others still can plunge into the water to catch fish or, hunting in pitch darkness, can drop unerringly on to the squeak of a mouse or the rustle of a beetle.

The largest bird of prey of all is the Andean condor, which is 3.04m (10ft) from wing tip to wing tip – much too big to glide in through your garage doors! But the condor is a vulture and feeds mainly on carrion. The biggest killer must be the harpy eagle that lives in the tropical forests of America. Some may weigh up to 9kg (20lb), which is about as heavy as a bird can be if it is to be able to fly well. Despite the harpy's 2.4m (8ft) wing span it can weave amongst the great forest trees at speeds of up to 80km (50mph) to strike and kill even large, wary monkeys. But many birds of prey can fly much faster than this. A peregrine falcon, for example, diving headlong at a fleeing pigeon may be able to reach a top speed of 290km (180mph) or more.

None of the owls can match these daytime killers for speed or size but in their own ways they are equally deadly. The eagle owl – standing 762mm (2ft 6in) high and with a 1.52m (5ft) wing span – will tackle and kill other birds of prey almost as big as itself and it can certainly take other much larger creatures too. There is one record of an eagle owl killing a roe deer which was more than three times its own weight.

Right at the other end of the size range come the tiny falconets and the elf owl – 152mm (6in) tall hunters of insects. Small they might be, but they are every bit as agile and deadly in their way as any of their bigger relatives.

Far left: To us a wide-eyed charmer, the Asian spotted scops owl Otus spilocephalus *is none-the-less an efficient hunter.*

Left: Because they are so well adapted to their role as predators, many small birds of prey, such as this North American saw-whet owl Aegolius acadicus *can kill creatures almost their own size.*

Opposite page: Peregrines Falco peregrinus *(top left) have evolved as high-speed interceptors, able to strike down birds in flight. The African black sparrowhawk* Accipiter melanoleucus *(top right) hunts birds in woodland and has less speed but greater manoeuvrability in flight than the peregrine. Owls, such as this barn owl* Tyto alba *(centre left) have developed other skills: most hunt at dusk or in the dark, making leisurely, silent flight. The huge Andean condor* Vultur gryphus *(bottom) has massive, broad wings which enable it to soar effortlessly at high altitude.*

Evolution

We do not know very much about the origins of birds of prey. Unlike the giant dinosaurs, whose huge bones have survived as fossils through millions of years of the world's history, birds have small light skeletons which quickly get eaten or rot away when a bird dies. As a result, there are few fossil remains of birds which would help us to trace their history. It is known, however, that the first, rather bird-like creatures, called Archaeopteryx, existed at least 150 million years ago, although it was not much like the birds we know today. For one thing, it had teeth; for another, it seems unlikely that it could fly properly, but only glide from tree to tree.

By about 100 million years ago, there were certainly real birds in existence. They had the specially shaped, deep breast bones that birds need to hold the muscles that power their wings in strong flight. They had lost their teeth and had normal beaks.

After another 40 million years had passed, a wide variety of birds had come into existence, including kinds which we can recognize as owls and hawks. In the 60 million years since then, while some species have certainly become extinct and other new ones have appeared, we can guess that birds of prey in general have continued to perfect their way of life and their skills as hunters and killers.

Nowadays, there are about 134 surviving owl species living in the world and just under 300 species of all other kinds of birds of prey. Perhaps surprisingly, these two groups are not at all closely related. Just as two brothers or sisters won't have exactly the same skills and interests, so it is with all creatures. No doubt some of the first hunting birds could see a bit better in the dark than others. Their offspring would tend to be more like them than not, and so gradually one group would become night hunters and the others would keep to the day, each group growing away from the other. Owls perfected night vision to allow them to move silently around a dense woodland in which we would crash and stumble blindly. Their hearing became so accurate that some can pinpoint prey when they cannot see it. By contrast, the daytime hunters needed to see into the distance, so that an eagle's long sight is perhaps eight times keener than an owl's. In addition, they developed many special wing and tail shapes to enable them to fly fast and far.

Although they are unrelated, some members of these two groups look rather like each other. This is because they live in the same way. Some owls have learnt to hunt by day and appear very similar to hawks or falcons. A few of the daytime raptors – as birds of prey are also called – have learned to hunt in the dusk. Perhaps in the future, they will grow to look and live like owls.

Evolution ensures that different species do not directly compete with each other. This martial eagle Polemaetus bellicosus *(below, left) may spot a game bird some distance away across the African savannah and then make a low level approach at high speed to take it by surprise.*

Below right: The tiny pygmy falcon Poliohierax semitorquatus *shares the same habitat as the huge martial eagle, but it takes very much smaller prey.*

Opposite: The Malaysian eagle owl Bubo sumatrana *is one of twelve related species in the world which between them take a similar range of prey to that hunted by eagles: however they hunt in different ways and at different times.*

The Senses

The eyes are one of the most noticeable features of any birds of prey. They are large, often beautifully coloured and they seem to return your stare, unblinkingly. Sight is obviously of the greatest importance to any hunter. Without keen vision, there is every chance it would not even see its prey, let alone catch it. Most creatures which are hunted are themselves constantly on the look-out for danger. Many are adept at concealing themselves and are cautious about coming out into the open. Some have camouflage markings which help them to blend into the background. Others are able to rely on their own speed and agility for protection so they have to be stalked or ambushed before they have time to gather their wits and flee. This being so, you might expect birds of prey to have specially constructed eyes which would allow them to see things better than we can; this is indeed the case.

Birds' eyes, like our own, are more or less spherical. Light enters through the pupil and is focused by a lens onto the sensitive inside wall of the eyeball, in the same way as a slide is projected on to a screen. This part of the eye is called the retina and it is equipped with special cells which change light into signals which the brain can 'see' and understand. There are two sorts of these cells. One kind, called rods, are light-sensitive and important to animals which need to move about in poor light or darkness. The others are called cones and are essential to the sharpness of the picture and to record its colour.

Birds of prey which are designed for daytime living – the eagles, buzzards, falcons and so on – take advantage of the bright light of the sun, by having sight adapted for extreme sharpness of vision at long range. The lens at the front of the eye projects a large picture on to the retina. In turn, the retina is richly equipped with cone cells that produce a very crisp colour picture of even tiny objects. It seems certain that these birds have very much better vision than we do, and to improve their visual ability still further, two small areas of the retina of each eye (called the foveas) have even greater picture definition.

No-one yet knows precisely how well these birds can see but it is thought that a golden eagle sitting on a crag can spot a mountain hare perhaps four times as far away as you or I could. When it concentrates its gaze on the animal and uses its foveas, it is probably seeing it as well as we might through eight-magnification binoculars.

Given such powerful sight, it is certainly within the eagle's ability to see the hare, which is about 508mm (20in) long, more than 1.6km (1 mile) away. A big vulture cruising perhaps 610m (2000ft) above the ground will have no trouble spotting the body of even a small dead animal. When it starts to descend, another vulture perhaps 6.4km (4 miles) away will be able to see what the first one is doing, will guess what is happening and will also start to glide towards the meal. In minutes, birds from twenty miles away will be on their way, all having received news of the feast by their superb eyesight. Equally, a buzzard sitting watching on a post can spot a grasshopper hop more than 30 metres (100 yards) away. Even if the grasshopper was to keep quite still in all probability it wouldn't escape the bird's patient scanning of the scene.

For owls, the problem is somewhat different. Unlike most daytime hunters, they place a lot of reliance on their hearing, but they still need to see in the dark at least well enough to move around without bumping into things, which would damage them and also alert their prey. Of course, it is never truly dark out of doors. After nightfall, some of the sun's light still finds its way to the dark side of the earth. In clear weather the moon, or stars by themselves, give quite a lot of light and even when it is cloudy, there is still

Opposite: The facial disc of the long-eared owl Asio otus *contains its prey-sensing equipment. This consists of huge eyes designed to see in the dark and enormous ear openings that extend right round the side of the face beneath the feathers.*

Left: All birds have a transparent inner eyelid that they can close to protect the eye from damage when, for example, they are landing amongst dense twigs or subduing prey. This long-crested eagle Spizaetus occipitalis *is an African species which feeds on rodents.*

some light. Most of us, living in brightly lit towns or villages, are not accustomed to moving about in natural darkness but once our eyes adjust to the night and the iris opens out to let in whatever light is available, it is surprising how much we can see.

Owls are far better equipped than we are for night-time vision. The retinas inside their eyes are particularly well equipped with the light-sensitive rod cells and it has been calculated that their sight is up to one hundred times as sensitive as our own. If this is so, they can see as well on a moonlit night as we can in broad daylight and even on the darkest night, they can see quite adequately to fly confidently through dense woodland and to catch their food.

During the day, owls have to protect the sensitive interior of their eyes from the damage which might be caused by strong light. This they do by closing down the coloured iris so that the pupil becomes smaller. They also have a special transparent inner eyelid called the nictitating membrane which they can shut at will. All birds have these and use them mainly to protect their eyes from damage, for instance by closing them when alighting amongst dense twigs or when feeding their young. Some swimming birds use them as diving goggles and owls use them as sunglasses. Once they have adjusted to daylight, however, owls can see quite well and indeed some species hunt by day for preference. Those which live in high Arctic areas – the lands of the midnight sun – have no alternative but to hunt in almost continuous daylight during midsummer.

Perhaps the most striking thing about owls – even more than other birds of prey – is the way they can return a gaze. Other birds may cock their heads and seem to peer at you with one eye, but simply cannot stare directly in the way that a cat, an eagle or a person might. This is a very obvious and fundamental difference between creatures which hunt and those which are primarily hunted. The robin, the mouse or the hare – they all need good all-round vision. Their food is just under their nose, but danger may be anywhere, so they can see to the front, to both sides, quite a long way behind themselves and up into the air, all at one and the same time. As a result, they can keep a good look out even while they are eating. But the hunter's main need, on the other hand, is to judge the precise position of its prey before launching any attack.

Certainly there is little problem for the bird of prey in catching a grasshopper and still less in settling on to a dead donkey, but catching a mountain hare or a pigeon in

flight requires care and planning as well as speed and strength. If the quarry is too far away, there is no point in giving chase because it will gain cover and safety before the hunter can reach it. So first, the hunter must judge how far off it is. There are two ways of doing this and we use both of them ourselves.

By moving one's head from side to side or up and down, one can judge which things are nearer in a landscape, for example, because they seem to move relative to those further away. Owls in particular will often use this technique, bobbing and twisting their heads in order to pinpoint the position of something that interests them.

The other method depends on having binocular vision, which means the ability to focus both eyes on an object. You know that the nearer an object gets to you or you to it,

Though quite unrelated, barn owl Tyto alba *(above) and white-tailed kite* Elanus leucurus *(opposite, bottom right) share the binocular vision essential to all birds which need to judge distance precisely in order to grasp quickly moving objects.*

the more you must angle both eyes inwards to keep it in view, until eventually, if it gets too close, you go cross-eyed. This variation in eye angle gives the brain clues as to distance of the object. You can prove this for yourself by shutting one eye and reaching out your hand to try and touch something an arm's length away. You will find it much more difficult to judge the exact distance than if you looked at it with both eyes open. For men and monkeys, binocular vision allows precise use of the hands. In birds of prey – as in cats – it is perhaps of prime importance in the moment when they make contact with their prey, for they must at all costs strike or grasp accurately with their feet – any fumbling and the quarry may escape or even turn and fight back.

So that the visual picture will be as big and as finely detailed as possible, raptors' eyes are large and take up a lot of room in their heads. For example the snowy owl stands only about 61cm (2ft) high, but its eyes are about as big as a man's. However, they are fixed almost rigidly in their sockets and cannot be rolled from side to side. To compensate for this apparent disability, all such birds have flexible necks: owls can rotate their heads at least through three-quarters of a circle in order to look back over their shoulders. Thus they can 'cover their backs', for hunters can be hunted too, and they can also silently survey their whole surroundings without having to move.

While falcons such as peregrine Falco peregrinus *(below) and kestrel* Falco tinnunculus *(left) also possess binocular vision, their eyes are set more to the sides of their heads than is the case with owls. Unlike the barn owl, therefore, they do not need to rotate the head right round in order to look behind.*

Some birds of prey have strikingly coloured eyes. In many, the iris is brown, so that the whole eye looks rather dark, but some are brilliant yellow, orange or even red. The American king vulture has a black pupil surrounded by a white iris which in turn is encircled by a red rim. Not only do different species of raptors have differently coloured eyes; in some birds, eye colour changes with age, or the male and female of the same species have eyes of a different hue. This clearly has nothing to do with the efficiency of their sight, but what purpose it does serve, still remains a mystery.

Together with their keen sight, most birds of prey have very good hearing to help them in their hunt for food. This is particularly true of owls. Their ears are often enormous and especially tuned to pick up high-pitched squeaks and rustles of small animals moving through the undergrowth.

Owls' ears are not located in the two big tufts of feathers that some species have on their heads, but are situated around the sides of their faces. The ear openings found there, in some cases, form a semi-circle reaching from above each eye to below it. Wholly concealed beneath the feathers of the face, they are fitted with flaps which can be moved – like cupping your hand behind your ear – to help collect sounds and locate where they are coming from. In doing this, the flattish disc of feathers which covers most owls' faces may itself also help to concentrate noises, rather as a radar disc does.

To find out exactly where a sound comes from, birds have to solve two problems: they must establish both the direction and the distance. Get someone to make a clicking noise behind you, moving it 5–7.5cm (2–3ins) either side of your spine and up and down from your head to your feet and you will find that you can accurately locate the

sound source as it moves. This is because the sound arrives first, and may seem louder in the ear nearer to its source. The further apart a creature's ears are, the greater the time lag in the sound reaching the other ear – and so the easier it is to judge where it came from. This is an important reason why owls have unusually wide heads and in fact small species seem to have proportionately wider heads than their larger relatives, as if they were striving to get their ears ever further apart.

In many owls, the ear aperture on one side of the face is higher than the one on the other side. Sound rising from below or coming from above will therefore reach the nearer ear first. So, at the first squeak or rustle in the leaves or the undergrowth, the owl can judge just how far to left or right it must look: at the second, it knows just how far up or down to look. Often, it can probably make both calculations at the same time from only one

Above: An Indian white-backed vulture Gyps bengalensis *scans the ground for food: when it descends, other vultures far away will see it and come to share the meal.*

Experiments with captive long-eared owls Asio otus *(below right and opposite, bottom) show that they can capture prey in total darkness, using their acute hearing. However, the tufts of feathers on their heads are not ears, but give the bird a distinctive silhouette that may aid mutual recognition.*

Far left: The extraordinary colours of the eye and head of the American king vulture Sarcorhamphus papa *may be important for success in gaining a mate.*

Left: Unlike humans, birds blink with the lower eyelid. Another characteristic shared by all raptors is a large gape, illustrated here by a forest eagle-owl Bubo nipalensis *as it begins to cough up a pellet of its prey's fur and bones.*

Far left: From a perch, an American great-grey owl Strix nebulosa *listens patiently for any sound that will reveal the location of possible prey.*

sound. Then the eyes come into play, focusing on the spot the ears have pinpointed. They can probably see any further movement the quarry makes, but at this stage in the hunt, eyesight is not essential. Experiments made with captive birds suggest that, given a couple of brief squeaks to guide them, some species are able to catch their prey even in total darkness, which, in any event, is a situation that never arises in nature.

An owl, then, sits silently in a tree, reading the sights and sounds of the night as easily as we watch and hear television. One tell-tale squeak and the sensing head turns, probing the dark with great keen eyes and incredibly sharp ears. Another sound, or a minutely visible movement, and the bird leans forward, opens its wings and slips silently from its perch. Now it probably doesn't matter whether or not the prey is moving or making any noise because the owl has fixed its position with deadly accuracy and is gliding swiftly towards it. At the last moment, the bird swings its body so that the taloned feet come forward to thump down and grip the unsuspecting victim and, almost instantly, squeeze out its life. Frighteningly efficient and quick it may be, but it is also mercifully unexpected and generally painless.

Good hearing is not only helpful to birds which hunt at night. It also assists those which operate during the day, particularly if they seek prey which is concealed in deep cover. Harriers, for example, feed on all sorts of creatures that live in marshes, heaths, moorland and other open habitats. Because these places are clearly visible from the sky above, the animals that live there do their best to conceal themselves by moving around under the cover of plants – whether they are reeds or heather, grass or bracken. There is not much point, therefore, in a harrier sitting a long way off and watching for its prey. Instead, what it must do is fly low and quite slowly over the area, looking very carefully below it for tell-tale movement and listening for any slight sound that suggests a creature moving or trying to hide. Harriers not only have large ears that are designed to collect any small sound, but they also have the same sort of disc of feathers that owls have on their faces. This perhaps helps to confirm that the facial disc helps to collect and concentrate noises.

The somewhat dark and gloomy tropical forests, offering plenty of cover in which prey can hide, make them a habitat in which

Below: Hearing is not only important to nocturnal raptors, but also to those which hunt in the deep, year-round shade beneath the canopy of tropical forests. It is also an asset to birds like the Australian spotted harrier Circus assimilis, *which seek creatures that are hidden in the low, dense cover of grasslands and marshes.*

good hearing is important. Accordingly, some of the falcons which live in them have large ear openings. Interestingly they don't have facial discs but, instead, the feathers around the ear are stiff and upcurled, so may serve in a different way to help concentrate sounds. Not much is known about how these birds hunt as it is so difficult to watch them in their natural habitat. It seems likely though, that they chase their prey through cover and on the ground, unlike falcons elsewhere which hunt in open country and rely on good eyesight and high speed of flight.

Although all raptors have quite visible nostrils situated in the top of the beak, it seems that most of them do not have a very good sense of smell. Obviously animals such as foxes or lions, that move around and hunt on the ground, find a good scenting ability very helpful, because smells cling to vegetation and are also blown along by the wind. But birds moving high in the air obviously cannot make use of these scents in the same way.

There is one group of birds of prey, however, which has quite well developed olfactory organs and so can be expected to possess a reasonably well developed sense of smell. These are the vultures which live in North and South America. There is considerable uncertainty, in fact, as to how well they can smell things, and how they use whatever ability they have, but the assumption is that it helps them in locating the carrion on which they feed, particularly in wooded or forest areas where it may not be readily seen. Of course, this sort of food has a very strong smell once it does start to go putrid.

There is no evidence that other birds of prey – whether or not they feed on carrion – rely at all on an ability to smell it. The vultures that live in the rest of the world are not closely related to the American species and they have small olfactory organs. But they feed in open country and can therefore depend on their eyesight and on watching the behaviour of other creatures in order to detect their food. In fact, they usually find any carcass quickly and eat it while it is still fresh, before it begins to reek. Owls also seem to make no use of scent. Their sight and, more particularly, their hearing are obviously wholly adequate for their hunting. There is very little evidence of any species of owl feeding on carrion, which being motionless and silent is probably generally ignored by them.

Below left: Few birds have a good sense of smell, but the American turkey vulture Cathartes aura *has well-developed olfactory organs which may help it to find small items of carrion that are concealed by ground cover. Here, however, they are feeding at a large carcass, which they could easily see from afar.*

Below right: Typical vegetation of tropical rainforests, photographed in the eastern Andes in Ecuador.

Physical Features

All birds of prey, whether they hunt by day or by night, have hooked beaks. In most cases, these are not used to kill prey, but simply to tear pieces of meat from the fresh carcass. Raw meat is usually quite tough and, in the larger mammals at least, it is enclosed in a strong outer skin or hide which may be hard to penetrate. Birds with straight beaks find it difficult, therefore, to feed on flesh and indeed only a few have the ability either to eat carrion or to kill small or defenceless animals. The bird of prey has no such problem. It drives the hooked, pointed end of the upper mandible into the flesh of its prey, closes its beak so that it has a firm grip and then, with its feet firmly planted on the body to hold it still, gives a good tug. In this way, a raptor can rapidly pull off small chunks and swallow them whole or feed them to its young.

The beaks of different kinds of predatory birds do vary somewhat in shape and size, however. Some of the eagles have the biggest, heaviest beaks of all. This is because they eat fairly large mammals and have to break through a tough skin before they can begin to feed. They may 'cut up' a large carcass, removing the legs and head, and even breaking the body in two so that they can carry off the pieces and hide them to guard against future hunger.

Hawks and falcons both feed on other birds and so have lighter, shorter beaks because bird carcasses are comparatively fragile. There is one special difference between these two types of birds though. They both usually kill birds with their feet but a falcon will also normally break the neck of its prey by biting it. It can do this in flight, while holding the quarry in its feet and it may make it easier for them to subdue large prey. The upper mandible of its beak has serrations, called toral teeth, which are used for this purpose. Some other kinds of raptors also have these toral teeth but it is less apparent why they really need them.

Undoubtedly, the bird of prey with the most extremely hooked beak is the snail kite. Its upper mandible is so long, slender and deeply curved that it can slide it inside the shells of the large snails on which it feeds and winkle them out.

At the other extreme, the caracaras, which come from central and South America have bills that are only very slightly hooked. These birds seem to spend a lot of their time seeking food on the ground, where they pick up a wide variety of small prey. Perhaps their 'general purpose' beaks are best suited to the ground foraging they favour. However, caracaras are odd birds and it seems that they retain some very primitive characteristics which other birds of prey have lost. One disadvantage of a deeply hooked beak is that it makes 'chicken-style' pecking impossible, which is why birds of prey cannot turn over soil or leaf-litter to search for prey. Despite this, several species do manage to eat smallish beetles or termites without any trouble.

Owls' beaks vary in shape and size from species to species, but they lack the extreme shapes and forms of diurnal raptors simply because their nocturnal habits limit their food range to more conventional items than snails and caterpillars. One interesting point is that an owl's beak tends to slope downwards noticeably. A possible explanation for this is that it does not obscure the bird's vision, which it might do if it stuck out straight in front of the forward-facing eyes. While day-flying birds of prey usually pluck their food, removing feathers or fur before they eat, and then consume it bit by bit, many owls prefer to swallow their prey whole without even removing its outer coat. Barn owls use their beaks to crush the heads of small mammals before gulping them down in one swallow. Larger prey must be

Opposite page: The beaks of birds of prey. Barn owls Tyto alba (top) usually swallow small mammals whole, having first crushed the skull with their beak. The beak of the common caracara Polyborus plancus (below left) is only slightly hooked: as a result, it can peck up items, such as small reptiles, more easily than can species with deeply hooked beaks. The Everglades kite Rostrhamus sociabilis (inset top) has a deeply curved and pointed beak which is a specialized tool for dealing with its diet of large, aquatic snails. The beak of the Philippine monkey-eating eagle Pithecophaga jefferyi (bottom right) seems to be larger than necessary for the thin-skinned prey it likes.

Left: An African species, the lappet-faced vulture Aegypius tracheliotus has a huge, broad bill to penetrate the tough hides of large carcasses.

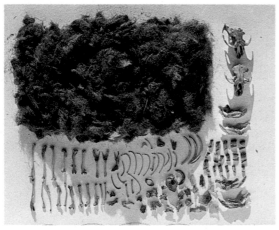

torn up before being eaten and so must food for the owl chicks which, at least while they are still very small, need to have their food torn up into tiny slivers by the mother bird.

Many birds, and perhaps all those that swallow indigestible material while feeding, later cough it back up in the form of dry pellets. In these will be found the fragmented, hard external skeletons of insects, the bones of small mammals or birds wrapped up in bits of their fur or feathers, and even the bristles of worms. Birds of prey, and in particular owls which swallow their victims whole, regularly produce these pellets. If the bird normally roosts in the same place, a huge pile of them may build up on the ground below, providing a good record of its food over a long period. The pellets can be softened in water and gently teased apart so that all the component parts may be clearly seen. Jawbones of small mammals can usually be identified to individual species and the hard parts of insects – particularly the wing-cases of beetles – may be recognizable.

Perhaps more than any other feature, it is their feet which distinguish raptors from all other birds. The other species use their feet for walking or hopping, for perching, swimming or climbing, but birds of prey have developed the use of their feet as the deadly weapons with which they kill their food. In handling a bird of prey, it is the feet, not the beak, that one has to be particularly careful about. Falconers wear long, heavy leather gloves in order to protect their hands and arms from the injury that could arise if a frightened or angry bird suddenly gripped hard and dug in its talons. It is from the habit of grasping their prey that birds of prey get their alternative name of raptors and as an extra aid to prevent prey from wriggling free, many of them have hard, fleshy bumps spaced at intervals along thin toes. These dig into the victim as the bird clamps its feet shut.

Birds of prey generally kill their prey by grasping it with their feet and crushing it, while driving in both hind claws like two curved daggers. Usually, the strike is aided by the bird's speed as it contacts its victim. Landing on small ground game, such as voles or mice, a large bird of prey like a buzzard or a tawny owl has to exert very little effort in making its kill, but a larger animal is a tougher proposition and some raptors kill mammals three or even four times their own size. Ideally, the bird comes in fairly fast and at the crucial moment before impact kicks out strongly with both feet to strike the prey hard with the force of its own momentum and the sharp muscular kick. The difference is that of simply ramming into someone full-tilt and making a two-footed flying kick – the way Kung-Fu experts do.

Often the result of the bird's attack – especially if it is unexpected – is to knock the prey down. Once thrown off balance, it is at a great disadvantage in any attempt to escape or fight back. The raptor's feet instantly squeeze hard, perhaps shifting as the bird seeks to stab a vital spot with its hind talons, and the struggle is quickly over.

Killing in this fashion demands very strong legs and feet and birds that take prey which is large and strong compared to their own size usually have short, stout legs, while their feet have shortish, thick toes. Contrast this with the airborne bird-catchers, like

Opposite, top left: The huge beak of the Steller's sea eagle Haliaeetus pelagicus *from north-east Asia gives a good indication of this bird's ability to eat large, tough prey. However, it is the powerful, crushing feet that make the kill.*

Long toes are useful to all raptors that hunt quick-moving creatures. They are possessed by both the lanner Falco biarmicus *(opposite, top right) and the American kestrel* Falco spaverius *(opposite, bottom right): both are falcons, and the former lives by capturing birds in flight over open, arid country while the latter preys mainly on small mammals in grassland.*

Opposite, bottom left: A pellet from a short-eared owl Asio flammeus, *teased apart to show the contents: it includes the skulls and jawbones of small mammals, as well as other bones and fur.*

This page, top: Most diurnal raptors have bare legs but booted eagles Hieraaetus pennatus *are closely feathered to the toes.*

This page, bottom: The harpy Harpia harpyja *has exceptionally powerful feet and legs.*

21

sparrowhawks. Their prey is not particularly strong, nor is it well able to defend itself, but it is quick and agile. So the sparrowhawk has slim, extra long legs which end in long-toed feet. Thus it has a really long reach and is able to snatch – often with just one foot – a small bird that is trying to dodge into cover.

Long legs have their uses in other situations as well: harriers, trying to grab elusive prey in dense ground vegetation such as heather, find it helpful to have a long reach. The African harrier-hawks actually have double-jointed legs which allow them to be specialists in searching in holes and crannies. They poke a leg into these and feel up and down and to either side, seeking out any hapless animal, such as a bat, nestling or squirrel, that may be lurking there.

Birds such as the chanting goshawks from Africa have long legs to give them agility in hunting on the ground – but the raptor with the longest legs of all is the secretary bird. It spends most of its time stalking around, searching for snakes which are one of its principal foods. It kills them by kicking and stamping on them.

A number of other birds of prey use their feet in unconventional ways. Honey buzzards – which live in Europe, Asia and Africa – feed extensively on wasp and bee grubs. These they obtain by digging out the nests from the underground cavities in which they are constructed. Ospreys live on fish and they are able to swivel round the outer toe on each foot so that they can carry their slippery prey with four talons dug in on each side of the body (an arrangement also preferred by owls, whatever prey they take). Ospreys are further aided in gripping fish by the many tiny spines which cover the undersides of their toes. Similar spicules are found on the feet of the Asiatic and African owls which also specialise in fish-hunting.

By contrast with other birds of prey, vultures do not need powerful feet because they feed largely on creatures which are already dead. Instead, their talons are quite small, making their feet much more suited to walking than those of birds like eagles. Clearly it is useful for vultures to be able to move quite agilely when many individual birds may be bounding about and competing for food at a single large carcass.

Birds' feathers are important to them for several different reasons. First of all, the feathers keep them warm. Right next to their skins, birds have a coating of fine down that provides a warm, insulating layer underneath their outer feathers. The outer feathers – which are called contour feathers because of the way they follow the shape of the bird's

Top: The pale chanting goshawk Melierax canorus *is partly a terrestrial hunter, taking lizards and insects, but it also hunts birds in flight.*

Left: A male European sparrowhawk Accipiter nisus *at a plucking station. Many birds of prey have preferred eating places to which they take their food.*

body – can be raised or fluffed up when the weather is cold so as to increase the thickness of the insulation surrounding the bird's body – like putting on an extra sweater or fluffing out the duvet on your bed. In hot weather, when the bird might become overheated, it presses its feathers down close to its body, thereby making the insulating layer as thin as possible, which means body heat can radiate rapidly through it. If this isn't sufficient the bird may open its beak wide and pant so that air circulates over the moist tissues and the evaporation helps to cool it down.

Birds which live in particularly cold climates often have feather-covered legs. This is true of some Arctic birds of prey, notably the rough-legged buzzard and the snowy owl. With the exception of most fishing owls, to which feathers would probably soon become a soggy inconvenience, almost all owls have feathery legs. Perhaps this is to provide them with extra insulation because they are active at night, when air temperatures are nearly always a lot lower than during the day. It is possible, too, that owls prefer to swallow their prey whole whenever possible because their feathered legs might

Opposite: The 1.2m (4ft)-tall secretary bird Sagittarius serpentarius *is perhaps the strangest of all raptors, with its enormously elongated shanks. It seeks its food on the ground, and kills snakes by stamping on them.*

Opposite, top: Silent flight is essential to owls attempting to surprise prey in the dark. The flight feathers of this tawny owl Strix aluco *have soft fringes that suppress the hiss of air over their surfaces and between the pinions.*

Opposite, centre right: Plumage must be kept in perfect condition if it is to insulate the bird from cold, protect it from minor injury and permit it to fly really efficiently. Here a North American bald eagle Haliaeetus leucocephalus *enjoys a vigorous bath.*

Many vultures have bare heads and necks so that they can reach into large carcasses when feeding without fouling their feathers. Shown here (opposite, bottom right) are Ruppell's griffon vultures Gyps rueppellii *and African white-backed vultures* Gyps africanus.

Only a few birds of prey have such striking and beautiful markings as the white-faced scops owl Otus leucotis *(opposite, bottom left) from Africa and the spectacled owl* Pulsatrix perspicillata *(right) of central and South America.*

otherwise become smeared and matted with blood as they tear up their food. However, such conclusions may be quite incorrect; there is, after all, one group of daytime birds of prey, the booted eagles, whose legs are closely feathered right down to the toes, but they have no need of special night-time insulation, nor do they swallow their prey whole.

The other purposes of raptors' feathers are more obvious. Overlapping each other as they do, they form a smooth impervious surface which readily sheds water. Not only do birds not get wet when it rains, but this surface also provides some measure of protection from the injury that must always be a risk to highly mobile creatures moving around amongst the whippy twigs and branches of trees. Birds of prey, of course, have an added danger of physical damage, since the prey they capture may struggle and fight back. Against large creatures, feathers give little protection but they do provide a defence against insect stings – important for honey buzzards digging up wasps' nests – and against venomous snakes – important for short-toed eagles and a number of other species.

Absence of feathering on the head and sometimes on the neck is a feeding adaptation which is most noticeable on vultures. Obviously, a bird which pushes its head right inside the gory rib cage of a dead zebra, for example, would soon get its feathers matted and foul. The bare skin of the vultures, although it looks unattractive, is actually a nice, hygienic arrangement for these birds which do an essential scavenging job.

Plumage may be a variety of different colours and even special shapes. For most birds of prey, a generally inconspicuous mottled brown colouration is probably desirable as it allows them to merge with their backgrounds and remain unseen. A few have taken camouflage to considerable lengths – the snowy owl's white plumage, for example, must help it to remain concealed against even patchy snow cover.

Some gyrfalcons – another Arctic bird – are also white but, interestingly, not all of them are so coloured. In several raptor species there are considerable variations in the colour of different individuals. For instance, common buzzards can be found in the complete range of shades from almost white with light brown markings to dark brown with only a few light streaks. No certain reason for this is known, but it would undoubtedly make it readily possible for particular birds to recognize each other at long distances, which may be helpful when

they are defending their hunting or nesting territories.

Recognition may be the reason why so many kinds of owls have ear tufts. These vary subtly from species to species in their precise shape, size and location and so give each owl that has them a distinctive head silhouette. Meeting in the dark, quick identification at a safe distance is important when the other bird could be your mate, or a potential competitor for living space and food, or even, quite possibly, an enemy fully capable of killing and eating you.

Hunting by night, owls depend less upon agility or endurance and more upon complete surprise to capture their prey. This means that they need to be able to move about quite silently. To help them do so their feathers are extremely soft – indeed the wing feathers actually have fine, furry fringes, which means there are no hard edges to buzz or hiss as they flap through the air. At the same time, their wings are quite large in relation to their body size, so that they only need to flap slowly; that too reduces the noise they will make and, as well as adding to their ability to surprise their prey, also makes it easier for them to listen to the sounds of the night as they move from place to place.

Flight and Hunting

Feathers are truly an incredible invention; they combine lightness with strength and they carry out a whole range of functions. It would not be unreasonable to say that their most important contribution to the evolution of birds is that they have given them the ability to fly. And to fly far better, further and faster than any other creatures. Without any doubt, these powers of flight are seen at their best in birds of prey.

As with all creatures, the more energy a bird uses, the more food it needs to eat. This fact is particularly important to any hunter – if it has to put too much effort into catching its quarry, it could end up hungrier than it began! The ideal situation for a bird of prey would be to be able to kill one adequate meal every day, with the minimum of effort. But life is not as simple as that. In general, catching large prey does require a fair amount of effort because it can probably fly or run quite fast itself and could also be strong enough to fight back. On the other hand, catching lots of small weak animals could require quite a lot of energy too, simply in searching for them all. This means that each species of bird of prey has had to reach some sort of compromise by hunting those creatures which will give an adequate return of food without a disproportionate expenditure of energy.

Birds of prey have devised quite a number of different methods of hunting successfully without the need to use too much energy. Some rely on surprise attack so that they catch their prey before it even knows it is in danger. Others will fly extremely fast over short distances in open country in pursuit of their prey, while others rely on superb manoeuvrability to catch fleeing prey ever amongst dense cover. Yet others have devised ways of flying which require hardly any use of energy at all, so that they can remain airborne for very long periods without becoming tired. Different kinds of raptor, therefore, have become specialists in different styles of hunting and their shapes – particularly the shapes of their wings and tails – have evolved to suit their individual needs.

Let's look first at falcons, which mostly specialize in catching other birds or insects in flight over rather open country – on moors and heaths, mountainsides and at the coast.

In these open places, their enemies can usually see them coming, so it is essential that they should be able to fly very fast to catch fleeing prey however hard it tries to escape. Their wings are long in proportion to the length of their body and they taper to a fine point: this means that, when necessary, falcons can flap their wings very quickly through the air and so accelerate fast, like a sprinter.

The merlin is one of the smaller species of falcon and preys mainly on birds like larks and pipits. When it is looking for them it will either fly low over the ground, suddenly appearing over a ridge to arrive amongst a startled flock on the other side, or else it will sit quietly on a rock or hummock and wait for suitable prey to appear. As soon as a likely target comes within range, the bird is off in rapid pursuit.

Many of the larger falcons adopt much the same method of hunting, waiting their moment until the prey is close enough for them to be fairly certain of making a kill. Such judgement is obviously a finely developed art, requiring experience and patience. If a falcon were to launch its attack too soon, there might well be a lengthy chase in which it could become tired before it had made the kill. So it waits until it is confident that the creature it is watching has come close enough to be overtaken in one quick, decisive dash.

Usually the chase is fairly direct, but some species will climb above their target and then swoop down on it from above. The peregrine has specialized in this mode of attack. It waits quietly, usually sitting comfortably on a crag or circling high in the sky and watches the passing world. Its choice of victim is wide – ranging from finches to small geese – with pigeons as a widespread favourite. Often, the peregrine already has the advantage of height but, if not, once a suitable bird comes within reach, it will first climb above it and then dive down upon it at top speed. It aims with hairsbreadth precision to strike the fleeing prey with its feet as it hurtles past. The talons slash the victim, ripping into bone and muscle and knocking it out of the sky. Sometimes the peregrine even has time to pull up in mid-flight, turn and catch the falling body before it hits the ground. Usually the dive is begun from 15–18m (50–60ft),

Opposite: The American turkey vulture Cathartes aura *normally hunts by high-speed gliding. This allows it to cover large distances with minimal effort in its search for food.*

above the target and over a long distance peregrines can reach incredibly high speeds. Nobody has yet managed to time one really accurately but a maximum estimated speed of 290km/h (180 mph) could well be guessing on a modest side.

The peregrine is very much a specialist bird-killer, but most other falcons will also take mammals or insects, or both. In hunting insects, neither great speed nor endurance is essential, though hobbies show great co-ordination and agility as they hawk about for big dragonflies. Nor is the hobby a slow bird, being quick enough to capture swallows and even swifts. It has a habit of eating small prey on the wing, by holding it up to its beak in one foot.

While falcons are generally the experts at catching prey in flight, some other kinds of birds of prey have adapted to a similar lifestyle. Probably the most unusual is the bat hawk, which is actually a kind of kite. Unlike its kite relatives, many of which are

Far left: American swallow-tailed kites Elanoides forficatus *possess great aerial agility which enables them to feed on large flying insects and even to drink without landing. The black kite* Milvus migrans *(left) has a less specialized wing and tail shape, so that, while it retains reasonable manoeuvrability in flight, it is also able to soar economically on rising air currents.*

Centre: Eleonora's falcon Falco eleonorae *breeds on Mediterranean coasts and islands during the autumn, and rears its young on small birds captured as they migrate into Africa.*

Opposite: The white-headed vulture Aegypius occipitalis, *like all its relatives, has huge, broad wings and a short, broad tail. These enable it to float on rising air currents and remain aloft for long periods, with little expenditure of energy, while it searches for carrion.*

Left: Many birds of prey will feed on swarms of flying insects even if they do not normally find insect hunting worthwhile. Here black kites Milvus migrans *and the lanner falcon* Falco biarmicus *combine in pursuit of flying ants.*

carrion eaters and hunters of a variety of smallish creatures, the bat hawk specializes in feeding on bats and birds such as swifts and swallows. Largely active at dusk, when bats are emerging from their daytime roosts, the bat hawk has only a short period of time in which to capture enough food to last it for another twenty-four hours. As a result, it has evolved a falcon-like shape for swiftness of flight and it has a very large, gaping mouth so that it can gulp down much of its prey whole. In this way it does not waste time carrying it to a perch to eat in a more leisurely manner.

Most kites are agile fliers, attractive to watch, but the swallow-tailed kite is in a class of its own. Its long, forked tail is constantly in motion, opening and shutting like scissors: when the ends are spread they probably act like an extra wing, making it possible for the bird to fly very slowly. Certainly it has remarkable manoeuvrability. Hunting and feeding entirely on the wing, swallow-tailed kites take large insects and pick the contents out of other birds' nests. They do not even land in order to drink, but scoop up water open-beaked as they skim just above the surface.

Many birds of prey take insects, particularly in the tropics where they are large and plentiful. Even tawny eagles will sit and gorge themselves on swarming locusts or termites when the opportunity presents itself. At the other end of the size scale, tiny falconets hunt like flycatchers by sitting on an exposed perch with a good all-round view and waiting for an insect to zoom past. Then they dart out, grab it and return to the same perch to eat their prize, whilst waiting for the next one to fly by.

Of the true falcons, the kestrel is of particular interest, having become an habitual mammal-hunter. Although quite capable bird-catchers, most kestrels feed mainly on voles and mice – creatures which, at least by day, spend as much time as possible under cover, either in their tunnels or well down amongst the tangle of vegetation and fallen leaves that carpet the ground. To find them therefore requires not speed and agility, but patient and meticulous scanning of the ground for any small, revealing movement. Ideally, this is best done from a perch, but kestrels have perfected another method: they have mastered the art of hovering, which allows them to search for their prey in open country.

Facing the wind, they match their forward speed so precisely to the backward movement of the air that they can remain stationary about 9m (30ft) above the ground –

or at least, their heads can. If you observe closely you will see that as the wings flap and the tail fans and closes again, the bird's body is swinging, rising and falling as it adjusts itself to the gusting air, but throughout it manages to keep its head as motionless as if it was nailed on to the sky. The purpose of this whole operation is to provide a stable 'viewing platform' for the bird; the eyes must be stationary if they are to see things clearly. And the undoubted reward of having developed this special skill is that kestrels can hunt small mammals in open country where many other would-be competitors cannot function properly because there are no perches for them.

While the kestrels have brought hovering to a fine art, so much so that many of them hardly hunt in any other way, plenty of other raptors attempt it with more limited degrees of success. Many buzzards can hover for long periods where the strong upward movement of air over a ridge gives them a wave of wind on which they can balance, but without such assistance, they can only hover for a few seconds before they lose control or become tired. Eagles, too, will float steadily on a standing wave of air and the short-toed eagle actually can hover quite well. However, this eagle is mainly a snake-eater and so it does not compete with kestrels in any way.

A surprising number of birds of prey do live on snakes, which are much more nu-

Left: Buzzards and eagles are broad-winged raptors, able to soar for long periods on rising air currents. An augur buzzard Buteo augur *wheels slowly over the African forest roof, quite possibly flying for pleasure.*

Below: A pair of Verreaux's eagles Aquila verreauxi *in effortless, gliding flight. This species lives mainly on hyrax – rabbit-sized animals that inhabit rocky African hills. Though eagles in flight usually seem to move in a leisurely way, they can move extremely rapidly once they sight prey. Then they descend to strike in breathtaking dives.*

Right: A black breasted snake eagle Circaetus gallicus pectoralis *returns to its nest with a snake, half-swallowed, dangling from its beak. Living in Africa, where snakes are active year-round, this bird has no need to migrate, while snake eagles that breed in Europe must move to Africa in winter.*

Below: Eagles, in particular, spend long periods soaring high in the sky apparently just for enjoyment or – like this tawny eagle Aquila rapax *– sitting idly until they feel hungry again.*

merous in hot countries than in temperate ones. Whilst it requires no special agility to hunt them, it may be necessary to take some care in dealing with them once caught because, so far as is known, birds are not immune to snake venom. It seems they rely on the protection given by their feathers and by special bite-proof scales on their legs. As an added precaution, the bird mangles the snake's head as soon as it is caught. Smaller snakes are sometimes swallowed in flight and it is not an uncommon sight to see a bird flying along with the tail-half of a long snake hanging from its beak, while the front end is securely down in its stomach!

The art of hovering offers one solution to open-country hunting, but the harriers have developed another way of operating in this type of habitat. They rely on slow, low-altitude flight to give them plenty of time to look and listen for their prey. Although they appear to be biggish birds, their bodies are actually quite small and light. Their appearance of size comes from their long tails and long, rather slender wings – which are not unlike a 90–120cm (3–4ft) span model glider in shape. Because they are very light

Left: Because they have large wings relative to their small body size, harriers, such as this African marsh harrier Circus ranivorus, *can flap along slowly at low altitude for long periods without tiring while they carefully search the ground for small, concealed prey.*

Below: Short-eared owls Asio flammeus *have adopted a mode of hunting similar to that of harriers and also have long wings and buoyant flight.*

and have large wing surfaces, they seem practically to float along and the fact that so little effort is needed makes it possible for them to remain airborne for long periods without fatigue. It has been calculated that a harrier may fly about 180km (100 miles) every day. Such a distance is necessary to a creature which may have to search for ages before it finds enough small prey items to satisfy its needs.

In addition, the harrier's wing shape allows it to fly very slowly and often simply to glide along with its wings outstretched and slightly raised in a shallow vee, so it can peer closely into every tussock and every drift of dead leaves as well as listening carefully for any tell-tale sounds. It will meticulously quarter one area of ground before moving on to the next, and should something move, the bird will wheel round instantly and drop into the vegetation, its long legs outstretched to reach in amongst the stems and make its kill. Not only small mammals, but also reptiles, insects and birds may be caught in this way.

The fact that harriers are much bigger than kestrels and have developed this different hunting technique, makes it probable that they do not seriously compete with one another for food. In any event, harriers are likely to spot and catch quite different, generally bigger, prey items. The various harrier species each have their own particular choices of habitat and prey so that, even when two or more kinds live in proximity there is little competition. Instead all

The bateleur Terathopius ecaudatus *is a high-speed, low-altitude scavenger that covers great distances in its search for small dead creatures. Almost tailless, it manoeuvres by canting its wings and body from side to side, and its unique shape makes it very easy to identify.*

the available food supply is shared out fairly evenly. A study of Montagu's and marsh harriers found nesting near each other, showed that Montagu's harriers hunted within 2–3 kilometres (1–2 miles) of their nest sites, whereas marsh harriers ranged much further afield – up to 11–13 kilometres (7–8 miles).

It is interesting to compare the harrier's build and hunting method with those of the short-eared owl – a day-flying species that has adopted the same mode of life. Although these birds are in no way related to one another, they have much the same wing shape and flying style, both quartering the ground and using their sight and hearing to detect prey. Another day-time hunter, the northern hawk owl, by contrast, has developed similarities with falcons, such as long pointed wings and a long tail. However it does not seem to go in for high speed chases, preferring instead to hover or pounce from a perch onto mammals or swoop down after small birds.

Contrasting completely with harriers, the bateleur of Africa is one bird of prey which does its hunting by high-speed scanning. With a 1.8 metre (6ft) wing span and almost no tail, it flies at about 55–80 km/h (35–50mph) and steers by canting its wings from side to side – like someone walking along the top of a wall and keeping his balance with outstretched arms. It seems that bateleurs do not flap their wings very much and their method of flying is rather like that of some sea birds, which have developed a technique of using small air currents to maintain easy rapid flight. The bateleur feeds largely on small dead animals and this is probably why its hunting method differs so much from a harrier's. Its food, after all, is much easier to see because, being dead, it is not trying to hide! The bateleur, therefore, can fly faster without the danger of missing anything. That it is able to fly swiftly is important, for as there are undoubtedly fewer dead creatures than live ones around, if it did not cover sufficient ground, it would not obtain enough to eat.

Birds which feed on larger prey that is correspondingly easier to see, do not need to scan the ground from close range. Instead they can climb high into the sky where they have the advantage of being able to look over a very large area. This is the way buzzards, eagles and vultures in particular operate, and they have developed wing and tail shapes that allow them to soar with little or no effort at all by using natural rising currents of air.

As you will know if you have ever held your hand over a fire or a central heating vent, warm air rises. Exactly the same thing happens out-of-doors during the day. Even if it is cloudy, enough of the sun's heat filters through to warm the surface of the ground and in turn some of this heat is given off into the air near to it. The warmer air then begins to rise as bubbles or currents, which are called thermals. Birds such as eagles will enter a thermal during the course of their flight and then glide round and round in circles with their wings stretched out stiffly while the rising air moves past them and lifts them little by little up into the sky.

Birds that habitually use thermals to soar through the sky, have long, broad wings that end in long, primary feathers. These spread out separately like the fingers of a hand, which, it is thought, may reduce turbulence at the wing tips as they pass through the air and so make flight smoother and more efficient. Most of these birds also have short, broad tails which they can spread out like a fan. This increases the area of feathers against which the rising air can push. But how well a bird can soar depends on how heavy it is in relation to the size of its wings. A light bird with a big wing span can rise up faster on thermals than a heavy bird with the same size wings and a lighter bird can also use small thermals that occur in the early morning or evening, when the sun is not so hot as in the middle of the day.

As the lifting power of thermals depends on the sun's heat, big, soaring birds are at their most effective in hot countries. But good, strong rising currents of air are also present in hill or mountain country, because the shape of the land forces the wind up in great waves over the tops of the ridges. This makes it possible for birds like golden eagles to stay in mountain country throughout the year, even when the weather conditions mean that the air is far too cold for thermals to start working.

When soaring birds want to move across country, they do not need to flap their wings strenuously. Instead they simply rise up in one thermal and then make a long, shallow glide to the bottom of another one, where they can slowly wheel up again and repeat the process. When they sight their prey, they can descend extremely quickly by folding back their wings and tipping over into a high-speed dive.

Although they look ungainly and even unlovely on the ground, vultures are quite beautiful to watch in soaring flight. Some seem so big and broad-winged in the sky that they look almost like flying carpets. One of them, the Andean condor, is the largest of all flying birds with a wing span that sometimes exceeds 3m (10ft).

Vultures mostly soar high in the air and scan the ground beneath for any dead creatures. They may get clues as to where the next meal lies by seeing smaller scavengers such as crows and kites congregating around something which is hidden from their own view. Once one vulture starts to descend, another will soon spot it. Such a chain reaction quickly collects birds from a wide area, to squabble over the kill.

Far right: Vultures are essentially birds of hot lands where thermals permit effortless soaring flight and where the carcasses of large animals provide food. Usually, several different species gather at a carcass and each feeds on different parts; the white-headed vulture Aegypius occipitalis, *for example, takes hide and sinew, while others, like the white-backed vulture* Gyps africanus, *feed on the softer parts.*

Right, above: The hooded vulture Necrosyrtes monachus *is one of the smaller African vultures, often seen feeding on scraps dropped by the larger species at a carcass.*

Centre: Typical dry savannah of Africa, where the sun's heat provides thermals to aid birds' soaring flight.

The squabbles of vultures, however, are part of a well-evolved and successful plan. Different species will feed on different parts of a big carcass. Lappet-faced vultures, with their heavy beaks, can break through the hide of a thick-skinned animal and will feed on bits of outer skin or tear tough meat from the bones. The griffon vultures are meat-eaters whose bare heads and necks allow them to feed right inside the rib cage without getting their feathers dirty. The smaller Egyptian vulture has only a bare head (its neck is feathered) because it picks at smaller fragments dropped from the feast. So although all these birds appear to fight over a kill, no real damage is done. Generally, new arrivals threaten to attack birds which are already present and feeding. The attacker usually wins and thus the maximum number of birds get their chance to feed.

A long-winged and long-tailed vulture – the lammergeier – is found in mountainous country. This beautiful and skilful flier is fully feathered on its head and neck and has a scoop-shaped tongue which it uses to extract marrow from the bones of dead animals. In some cases lammergeiers have been known to carry large bones up into the sky and then drop them so that they split open on the rocks below and the bird can get

Above: The Egyptian vulture Neophron percnopterus

Left: A lammergeier Gypaetus barbatus.

Opposite top: Many birds of prey, like this lizard buzzard Kaupifalco monogrammicus *hunt from perches.*

Opposite, right: Capturing a small prey item, this augur buzzard Buteo augur *decelerates at the last moment by spreading its wings and tail, as it simultaneously throws forward its feet.*

Opposite, far right: A common buzzard Buteo buteo.

at the marrow inside the bone.

Perhaps even cleverer than the lammergeier, the Egyptian vulture has joined the exclusive and very small number of birds which use tools. It has learned that it can break open ostrich eggs by throwing stones at them with its beak. Australian aborigines claim that the buzzard-kite does the same thing with emus' eggs.

Besides vultures, buzzards and eagles will also take carrion and many species indulge in piracy, attacking and robbing other raptors of their food. Fish eagles are particularly well known for their raids on ospreys that are carrying fish, so that inexperienced young birds may have a difficult time until they learn to hang on tightly to what they have caught! It is difficult to know whether the aggressor would really press home its attack to the point of coming to grips with the other bird because the latter will usually give up its catch without much delay once the pirate gets too close.

But while they do not scorn an easy meal, eagles are versatile and powerful hunters and will take birds, fish and mammals including, for example, antelopes that are three or more times their own weight. Some can soar for long periods at a great height and then descend in a moment, diving at speeds easily in excess of 200km/h (120 mph) and perhaps nearly double that. Their mastery of high winds is amazing and they can fly in conditions when all other birds are grounded.

In hunting mammals and birds, eagles use cunning and their knowledge of the ground as much as their speed and power. An eagle which spots distant prey from high up and far off may make quite a round-about approach to it, coming in fast and low from an

unexpected direction, with talons spread, to smack into the startled victim before it has time to flee. Birds are mostly taken on the ground, although some eagles can and do make aerial captures. So great is their skill, that it seems as though eagles can kill food just about whenever they feel like it provided that prey is reasonably plentiful.

It seems that fish eagles living in the tropics have an easy life, so plentiful are the fish that bask near the water's surface all day. When hungry, they can simply make a leisurely flight out over the water and then glide down to lift the catch from the surface, with no more trouble than getting wet feet. Unlike fish eagles, ospreys are much more vigorous and energetic hunters. Instead of gliding in, they will check and hover right over a fish and then plunge-dive feet first and with wings raised over their backs. Sometimes one will vanish almost completely beneath the water, but a single vigorous sweep of its wings lifts the bird to the surface and with the next flap it is airborne, the fish securely clutched in both feet. Occasionally, fish eagles or ospreys will over-estimate their ability and grapple with a fish that proves too big to lift. They may simply hang on to it and work their way into the shallows, where it can be dragged ashore and finally dispatched.

One fish eagle has assumed a most unusual life for a bird of prey. It feeds largely on the husks of the nuts of oil palms in Africa. When it finds a ripe tree, it will return to it every day until it has eaten all the husks. Its name, the palm-nut vulture, is misleading because it is not a vulture at all and will, in fact, sometimes feed on fish and shellfish.

Several kinds of eagle have taken to life in forests – including one of the strongest of all flying birds – the harpy. Among the most impressive killers in nature, this rare bird is fully worthy to stand alongside the wolf and leopard as a masterpiece of hunting perfection. The harpy is a robust, heavily built bird, weighing up to a top limit of about 9kg (20lbs). Its wings are broad and rounded, spanning nearly 2.5m (8ft). The bird's head is a ferocious mask, with a divided crest that resembles two horns. Deep-set and piercing eyes stare boldly from either side of a strong and deeply hooked beak. Master of life in the tree-tops of South American tropical forests and equipped with remarkably thick legs and strong feet, the harpy hunts monkeys, sloths and other arboreal mammals. Very little is known about its life in the wild but it is believed to be able to glide between the tops of the trees at speeds of up to 80km/h (50mph). Not surprising therefore, that it

can arrive with terrifying suddenness, unannounced and unwelcome, amongst a troop of even the most sharp-eyed and nervous monkeys.

Although they are vastly different in size, harpys and hawks are basically the same shape. This is because they both need to be highly manoeuvreable in order to pursue fleeing prey in and out of close-set tree trunks, round dense bushes or through the interlaced branches of the tree-tops. To help them they both have long, strong tails which are in fact very efficient rudders also to steer them round tight corners even at high speed. Their wings are rather short and rounded (a complete contrast with the falcon's long, pointed wing shape) so that they can pass easily through narrow gaps without reducing speed. Hawks are short distance sprinters and like so many other raptors, they rely on cunning to get as close as possible to a victim, unnoticed. They will not often persist in a long chase.

The goshawk, one of the largest members of this group, is renowned for its skill and determination in hunting. Like other hawks, it spends much time sitting quietly and half-

concealed, waiting for unsuspecting prey to come to it. It attacks birds and mammals and will happily tackle species larger than itself. Once it has established a firm grip, it hangs on determinedly, stretching back to keep its head out of the way of flailing limbs until its talons find a vital spot and the struggle ceases.

All hawks are crafty in the use of cover in order to stalk a potential victim until they get close to it. A goshawk or a Cooper's hawk that spots a squirrel moving about in a tree across a clearing is too clever to try a straight attack, knowing that the squirrel would reach cover first. Instead, it slips away and approaches slowly and cautiously, working through the surrounding tree-tops, until it is close enough to launch a high speed attack at such short range that the squirrel's chances of escaping are reduced to a minimum. Sometimes the squirrel may not even see it coming until the hawk's claws stab into its back. If a squirrel is alert enough and tries to escape, the hawk may pursue it through the branches, screaming angrily at it so as to terrify and confuse it still further.

The smaller sparrow-hawks, which mostly take birds such as finches and tits, are most often to be seen hunting down a hedgerow or a line of trees, or round the edge of a patch of scrub. They will fly low so that they cannot be seen from the other side and then suddenly swing up and over to burst in amongst the small birds feeding unsuspectingly there. Some hawks will hurtle up to a patch of cover as though about to dive into it, then whip around it to fall upon the small birds that are hurriedly leaving by the back door.

However, small birds are not always so easy to catch. They are generally very observant and will warn each other if they see a bird of prey which might be after them. Interestingly, their reaction to falcons and hawks is quite different from the way they treat owls. If they see a hawk, they utter high-pitched calls. Many different species have similar hawk alarms, which is very useful, for whatever bird gives the warning, all others will understand it. It is also thought that it is difficult for a hawk to judge the direction from which such thin sounds come, which is obviously important because if hawks always found and killed the bird that gave the alarm, the warning would be completely counter-productive.

The way small birds deal with owls, in particular those they find roosting, is to gather round and 'mob' them, while calling loudly between themselves. They are usually careful not to get too close, but clearly feel

Many different kinds of raptors are called 'hawks' but strictly a hawk is a bird adapted for hunting through woodland cover, possessing relatively short rounded wings and a long tail. Examples are the sharp-shinned hawk Accipiter striatus *(opposite, bottom) and the goshawk* Accipiter gentilis *(right, top). The Galapagos hawk* Buteo galapagoensis *(opposite, top) and the red-shouldered hawk* Buteo lineatus *(opposite, centre) are in fact both buzzards. They are insufficiently agile to catch birds regularly and usually hunt from perches or from slow circling flight, so taking most of their prey on the ground. Dark chanting goshawks* Melierax metabates *(right, centre) are largely terrestrial predators. The hawk owl* Surnia ulula *(right, bottom) has adopted daytime hunting habits and has more pointed wings and a longer tail than other owls.*

that the owl is not much of a danger provided that all the birds in the area know where it is. It is said that small birds will avoid a particular area for several days after an owl has been mobbed there.

Compared with the great variety of hunting methods evolved by the birds of prey that are active by day, the owls that fly only at night, are strictly limited in the ways in which they can capture prey.

Because almost no other birds are on the wing during the hours of darkness, no nocturnal owls hunt in the same way as falcons or hawks. Because there are no thermals after sunset, none of the owls soar like eagles or buzzards. In any event, owls would lose the advantage of their special night-time senses if they were to fly high.

Only one or two species of owl are thought to take any interest in carrion. Generally, they hunt either by flying low and silently like a harrier, or by sitting and waiting for something edible to come along – a method that all birds of prey use at one time or another. It is silence, rather than speed or agility, that is undoubtedly the owl's greatest asset so most of them have rather rounded wings and buoyant, fairly slow flight.

The range of prey taken by owls is surprisingly great. Eagle owls can best creatures up to three times their own weight, including jackals, foxes, cats and small antelopes, and they will also kill other birds of prey including buzzards and even peregrine falcons. Many owls manage to catch birds at their roosts when they can see little and are largely helpless. Many species also take frogs but only a few catch fish and no nocturnal species hunt snakes, which are safely underground at night. Insects are also a common prey and species such as the little owl feast on earthworms when they are active on the surface in damp weather.

Nearly half of all kinds of owls regularly hunt by day or in the dusk as well as at night but, in spite of this, they have not yet evolved far from the hunting methods of their wholly nocturnal relatives. Only a few, like the northern hawk owl and the short-eared owl could be regarded as serious competitors with the diurnal raptors.

Perhaps to offset the apparently limited variety of ways in which they hunt, different kinds of owls reduce the competition between themselves by tending to favour different sizes or kinds of prey. A study of tawny, Ural and great grey owls living in the same area showed this very well. Tawnies and Ural owls of a similar size took about the same number of small mammals but the larger, stronger-clawed Ural owls took many more larger mammals than tawnies. Instead, tawnies caught a surprisingly high total of birds. Great grey owls, though bigger even than Ural owls, have weaker, rather slender toes and live almost entirely on small mammals. However, they were not

really competing with either of the other two species because they were active in the daytime, at which time tawnies were always roosting and Ural owls only hunted occasionally.

It is obvious that an intimate knowledge of the land over which they hunt is extremely important to at least some species of night owls. If they know every part of an area, they can move through it swiftly and efficiently, concentrating their attention on those places where experience tells them they are most likely to find prey. This is particularly important when food for every creature is at its scarcest – at the tail-end of winter for example. Then, any hunter that depends on catching numbers of other animals to keep itself alive daily stares the danger of starvation in the face. Birds like tawny owls hold individual territories, jealously driving out interlopers – any young bird which has not found a vacant patch and learned it well by the onset of winter is doomed to die of hunger.

Above and left: The little owl Athene noctua *feeds mainly on small creatures such as insects and worms, but it will take rodents and sometimes kills birds of nearly its own size. Such versatility enables most owls to remain in their breeding grounds during the winter months when food is in relatively short*

Migration

During the winter months, except in the Tropics, temperatures drop, the days are short and the nights long. Few plants grow at all and none produce seeds or fruit. This means that there is only a small amount of food available for plant-eating insects or animals and, thus in turn, for the flesh-eaters which prey on them. In spring, as the days become longer and the sun strikes warmer, the land too warms up and plant growth begins again, providing food for more and more creatures as the summer progresses. This is the time in which they can all breed because there is food to spare for all the new, young mouths. When the autumn comes, food once again becomes scarce and there are many more creatures competing for it than there were in spring, before the breeding season began. Great numbers of animals, therefore, will die during the winter unless they can avoid its lean months. Some creatures do so by hibernating. Another alternative is to move away, but for most animals, this is impossible because they cannot travel fast enough.

Few mammals and insects – perhaps not even many fish – make long distance migrations. Birds as a group are very fortunate because flight gives them the ability to move rapidly over very long distances. This means they can choose whether to stay or move away when winter comes. As a result, many species have become regular migrants, wintering in one place and spending summer somewhere quite different. Indeed, for some kinds of birds, there is no such season as winter because, having spent six months in the spring and summer in the northern half of the world, they then follow the sun and fly off to enjoy the same pleasant conditions in the south.

Migration has its dangers: a sudden change of wind can blow birds far off course so that they become totally lost, maybe drown at sea or die of thirst in a desert area. But the rewards of success are great and they allow birds to enjoy the richness that sunshine and rainfall bring to the earth, the year round.

Only one kind of habitat is almost unaffected by this vast ebb and flow of winged life. In the tropical forests, conditions change very little from season to season: there is neither winter cold nor summer drought, so of course there is no need for birds to leave. Equally, there is no spare room or extra food for visiting birds to exploit, so the birds that occur in tropical forests – including many kinds of raptors – are entirely resident. But outside these areas, birds of prey are often migrants, particularly if they feed on creatures which are hard to find or even unavailable in the winter months or the dry season of the year.

Many birds of prey feed on insects, for example. The honey buzzard digs out wasps' nests from the floors of forests in Europe and western Asia. Lesser kestrels and red-footed falcons catch large numbers of big insects, such as dragonflies and beetles, while the European scops owl pounces on these creatures on the ground, as well as snapping them up in the air. With the onset of cold weather, such food is just not available at all – some adult insects hibernate but most die and the different species live on through the winter as eggs or grubs secure in the ground, in plant stems or bark, or under water. Snakes too go into hibernation, forcing birds like the short-toed eagle out of their homes in southern Europe and into the warmer conditions of Africa.

Birds of prey that hunt in wetland habitats may also need to move as winter comes. There are no frogs or stupid young birds for the marsh harriers or the black kites to snatch up in reed beds or around the margins of rivers, lakes and pools. Ospreys cannot break the ice to catch their fish and, even if the water is not frozen, the fish themselves tend to move into the depths where they are out of reach, rather than basking close to the surface as they do on warm summer days.

Some of the bird-hunting falcons depend on prey species which are themselves only present in summer – hobbys for instance take such migrant birds as swallows and martins, warblers and pipits. This gives them one strong advantage – when they are migrating, they can actually travel along the same routes as the flocks of birds on which they feed.

A few raptors take particular advantage of the migrations of small birds. Eleonora's falcon breeds in places like the Mediterranean islands through which huge numbers of small birds pass each autumn as they head towards Africa. Nesting very late, the fal-

Opposite: Ospreys Pandion haliaetus *are distributed widely in the northern hemisphere during the breeding season, but they leave these colder areas in the winter months as fish become much less active and harder to catch, even where waters remain unfrozen. European breeding birds winter in West Africa, many fishing in coastal waters off the mangrove swamps.*

cons are able to feed their young on this easily caught and briefly abundant supply of food. Then they themselves join the end of the migration and wing away to 'winter' in Madagascar.

However, by no means all migratory birds have to move very long distances in order to find reasonable living conditions. Rough-legged buzzards breed right round the tundra lands close to the Arctic Circle in North America, Europe and Asia. They feed mainly on lemmings but in the winter these little animals are secure in their tunnels beneath the snow, so the rough-legged buzzards must move away. Because they are quite accustomed to cold conditions however (their name comes from the feathering on their legs which helps to keep them warm) they have no great need to move very far and will stop as soon as they come across any reasonable food supply. In some years birds which have bred in Scandinavia will travel as far south as Britain to feed on voles but more often they find a tolerable wintering place closer to home.

The behaviour of these birds and of several other northern mammal hunters such as snowy and great grey owls, also varies from year to year. Small mammal numbers fluctuate considerably – they may be very numerous for a few years and then, having eaten themselves out of house and home, millions will die in a matter of weeks. The famed migrations of lemmings – when many drown in trying to cross bodies of water – are caused by these food shortages. The effect on the birds which feed on the creatures is equally dramatic. While lemmings and voles are plentiful, the birds breed well and their numbers rise steadily. Then after a few years comes the inevitable crash and all the birds must leave the area or starve in their turn. Suddenly, rough-legged buzzards and snowy owls will 'irrupt' and occur far outside their usual ranges. Even so, many will die and perhaps only a small proportion eventually find their way back to start the cycle anew.

In different places, birds may behave in different ways. For example, kestrels that nest in the far north must leave when the area is gripped by frost and there is no food. But in slightly better conditions, where food is to be found even if it is scarce, some individuals will leave and others will stay. And in a third area, which is largely frost-free and has plenty of small mammals still active, all the kestrel population may be resident year-round. Britain provides an example of such an area. Most European scops owls migrate to Africa, but the North

American screech owls, which are also insect hunters, mostly manage to stay in their summering areas in winter. They do this partly because they are adaptable enough to change their diet and take whatever is going, including small mammals and birds. Equally important, in the autumn, they lay in stockpiles of food in their roosting places and build up a good layer of personal body fat. If the weather gets really bad, they can cease activity and live on their stores for a while.

Even if birds do regularly migrate, in some areas they only need to undertake quite short flights in order to find favourable conditions, as we saw with the rough-legged buzzards. Similarly, a pair of peregrine fal-

Above: Rough-legged buzzards Buteo lagopus *hunt lemmings but tend to move out of their breeding areas in autumn. Hunting where no trees grow, they are more skilled at hovering than the common buzzard, which is mostly associated with woodland.*

Right: Although most birds can only live in the northern tundra during the summer months, a few have adapted to all-year-round life in cold climates. The camouflaged plumage of the snowy owl Nyctea scandiaca *gives special protection against heat loss from the feet and around the beak. Feeding on lemmings, these birds only need to move when food supplies become short and they do not make regular migrations.*

Right, below: Typical summer scene in the mountains in Stekkenjokk, Lapland, in the northern tundra.

cons breeding on an upland crag in Wales, where they would probably feed on medium sized birds such as pigeons, might need to move away with the onset of hard weather. Then no more than an hour's flying could bring them to a coastal estuary packed with wading birds, which would provide abundant and easily caught food until the spring.

Apart from some of the insect feeders and the Arctic breeding species, there do not appear to be very many migrants among the owls. Probably the main reason for this is because it is important for a night-time hunter to be thoroughly familiar with the place in which it lives. The advantages, therefore, of moving to where food may be more plentiful are outweighed by the disadvantages of having to learn to find one's way around an unfamiliar territory.

In many of the hotter parts of the world, it is rainfall rather than cold weather which governs the lives of its inhabitants. Migration and breeding are closely linked with the fluctuations of food supply before, during and after the rains. Some species time their nesting so as to be rearing young when the rains bring new growth to parched lands. Others – which have become specialists at living in dry country – will actually move away in wet weather.

Where rains are infrequent and unpredictable, birds of prey may be nomadic, following food supplies from place to place. The letter-winged kite which lives in the arid interior of Australia may not breed at all in the bad years. Then, when the rains finally come in profusion, small mammals and insects suddenly become abundant and all the kites too can rear young. If the rains are widespread, the birds' numbers may greatly increase so that, once the glut is over and food again becomes scarce, like the Arctic species, they disperse and suddenly appear in new, unfamiliar areas almost all over Australia.

The regular migrations of the broad-winged raptors, such as eagles and buzzards, are one of the great spectacles of nature. Their long, broad wings allow them to fly with almost no effort as they rise up on one thermal and glide down on the next. Thermals do not occur over water, however, and so the birds either have to go round the edge of large areas of water or look for the shortest possible crossing. In some places, this means that huge numbers of birds are funnelled together in flight.

In Europe, buzzards and honey-buzzards coming from Norway and Sweden cross the Baltic by 'hopping' from island to island

Below: The great horned owl Bubo virginianus *is the largest owl throughout South and North America. It is found in almost all habitats including mountains, forests and deserts.*

Opposite, top: The short-eared owl Asio flammeus *is a daytime hunter found in open country right across northern Europe, Asia and America. It has also colonized large areas of South America and many oceanic islands.*

Opposite, bottom: Screech owls Otus asio *are a North American species which live on insects during the summer and mammals and birds in winter. Thus they do not need to migrate.*

until they reach Denmark. By going this way, they never have to cross any stretch of water much wider than 25 kilometres (15 miles). As they fly on down to the south, their numbers become swollen by many more birds and a greater variety of species. Once they reach the Mediterranean, the broad-winged species must bypass it either by going right to the western end and crossing at the Straits of Gibraltar, where only about 16 kilometres (10 miles) of water separate Europe from Africa, or to the east where only the very narrow Bosphorus divides Europe from Asia. Birds starting from yet further east – in western Russia – have to find their way round the Black Sea. Some come west to the Bosphorus while others fly round its eastern end, squeezing their way between the sea and the Caucasus mountains.

Bird watchers now regularly visit these places in autumn in order to count the birds passing by. This is the best way of checking whether their numbers are increasing or decreasing and thus determine whether the wildlife conservation organizations are doing sufficient to protect them. The greatest numbers seen in recent years were about 189,000 at Gibraltar, 76,000 at the Bosphorus and over 387,000 at the eastern end of the Black Sea.

On days when the weather is fine and large numbers of birds are moving at once, these migrations are truly spectacular to watch. The first birds start to appear early in the morning, as the sun warms the ground and the first thermals begin to rise. At first, they are mere dots in the sky, barely visible even through binoculars. Then one, two, a dozen are visible, until at last the horizon fills with streams of birds getting steadily closer and growing larger and larger. As they approach, they may gradually lose height, gliding down until they seem to pass just over your head. Sometimes, they will find a thermal rising near where you are standing and then the air will fill with circling shapes of dozens or perhaps hundreds of these big birds rising, spiralling one above the other on outstretched wings until they form a towering, whirling column high into the blue sky. Finally, those at the top begin to peel off and start the long, gradual glide away into the distance. One after another they go, often in such rapid succession that they are quite difficult to count and even harder to identify. Eventually the last of them will slowly wheel their way upwards, and the whole spiral seems to screw itself up into the sky as the birds rise and glide away from the top to form another spiral a mile or

Top: Map showing migration routes of birds of prey in Europe. Broadwinged birds of prey, such as eagles and buzzards, cannot make long sea crossings and so they travel round major water obstacles. Many thousands have been seen in autumn travelling via Gibraltar, over the Bosphorus and round the eastern Black Sea. Some birds of prey, including harriers, cross via Malta.

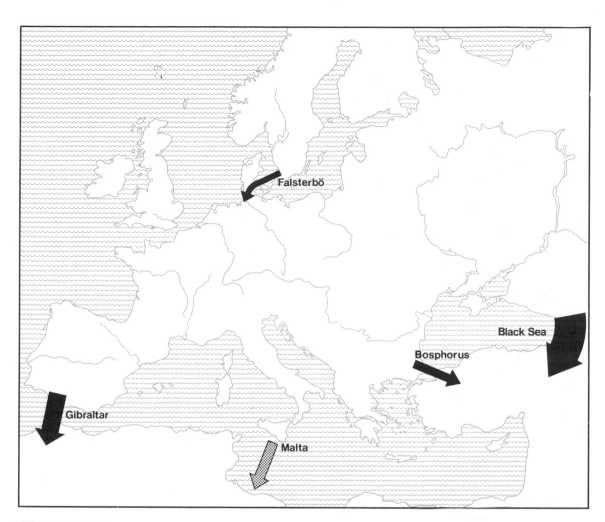

Opposite, top: Honey buzzards Pernis apivorus *breed in Europe and western Asia, but as they are specialist feeders on bee and wasp grubs, they must move south into Africa each autumn. Black kites* Milvus migrans *(bottom) have a much wider food range, hunting in wetland areas and also scavenging widely, particularly in African and eastern towns and villages. However, they are completely migratory throughout their range.*

Opposite, bottom: Great numbers of common buzzards Buteo buteo *travel through the mountain passes in eastern Turkey on their way from Russia into Africa each autumn.*

51

In summer, merlins Falco columbarius *(opposite, main picture) hunt small birds over open northern moorland and tundra, but when their prey migrates in winter, they must also move south. Long-legged buzzards* Buteo rufinus *(opposite, inset) from the steppes, and northern ospreys* Pandion haliaetus *(right, top) and black kites* Milvus migrans *(right, second from top) from the wetlands also have to migrate in winter. However, lammergeiers* Gypaetus barbatus *(right, third from top) may only move down the mountainside to escape the worst weather, while golden eagles* Aquila chrysaetos *(right, bottom) can often find food in winter without needing to migrate at all.*

more away down the length of the valley.

Of course, by no means all birds of prey that migrate have to go around rather than across water. Ospreys and harriers, for example, have large wings but their bodies are very light so they can flap their way along all day without getting tired, while falcons and hawks too have no problem at all in making sea crossings.

One of the mysteries about the migration of large birds of prey is whether they feed on their long journeys or carry out the whole flight – perhaps from northern Europe into southern Africa – without eating at all. We know that eagles can eat enough at one meal to last them several days, and we have seen that they do not use much energy when they are flying because they allow the air to do most of the work for them. It is clear, too, that there are also advantages in 'travelling light' because lighter birds can rise more quickly on the thermals than heavy ones, they can glide further before they need to rise again and they can take advantage of the small thermals that exist when the air is only slightly warmed early or late in the day. All this means that they can travel faster than the heavy birds can. The fact that migratory buzzards or eagles have never actually been seen to hunt is probably not all that significant. They are mostly observed at the concentration points where large numbers occur all at once and only a suicidal rat or rabbit would show its nose out of doors when there are hundreds of large birds of prey wheeling in the sky overhead!

Breeding Habits

Despite the dangers of migration, many birds clearly find it worthwhile because it allows them to breed and produce their young under the best possible conditions. Even for birds of prey, the nesting season is a difficult time when, unless they can catch a great deal of food, all their efforts will be wasted.

At first it can also be a dangerous time for them because male and female, which may have lived apart all winter, must get to know each other and learn to co-operate. In most birds of prey, the females are larger than the males and are certainly capable of injuring or perhaps killing them. The male bird therefore has to approach the business of courtship with some caution!

The first thing he has to do is to let interested females know that he is there and is the owner of a good territory, full of easily-caught prey and attractive places in which to nest and lay eggs. For the nocturnal owls, the best possible way of advertising themselves is to make a noise that will carry a long way, and this is what their hooting is all about. On a spring night in reasonably wooded countryside, it is fascinating to listen to the tawny owls calling. When one male hoots, another will respond and soon there is a sort of shouting match going on, spreading over the countryside as each male gives voice in turn. This singing is not only an invitation to the hen birds but also a warning to other males, which says 'don't try to come into this wood because I'm the owner here'.

Some hens have their own calls and will reply, which is obviously useful both for identification and for keeping in contact in the dark. In a few species, male and female blend their calls into a single duet.

Birds of prey that are active by day do not have to depend solely on their voices to advertise their presence, although many of them are very noisy and do call loudly and continuously. Their rather high-pitched voices sound a little strange coming from such big birds as eagles! Their main way of making their presence known, however, is to fly high in the sky, soaring, climbing and swooping in the most splendid aerobatics and relying on the keen eyes of any passing female to see them.

In many species, particularly the larger ones, male and female mate for life. Even if they are migrants that separate in winter, both will return to the same nesting area in spring. But, though they may be old acquaintances, they must still go through the courtship rituals, learning to accept the other's company and to begin to work together, as they must do if they are to succeed in rearing young. A male owl may dance in front of the female, stretching his body upwards as he sways from side to side and snaps his beak. Some vultures actually change colour in an effort to impress the female. The hooded vulture's pink face flushes a brighter red and the Andean condor's dark red head and neck turn to a yellow colour.

Male and female falcons carry out dramatic aerial chases, hurtling together and then rolling aside to pass each other with only inches to spare. Some soaring raptors perform exciting flying dances. Fish eagles link their talons and whirl through the air, tumbling over and over like swirling leaves.

Many male birds of prey will catch food and bring it to the females as a gift. As females are often bigger than the males, you

Opposite, top: Two American black vultures Coragyps atratus *delicately preen each other's neck feathers.*

Opposite, centre: The American burrowing owl Speotyto cunicularia *often breeds in old gopher holes.*

Opposite, bottom: A long-eared owl Asio otus *brings prey to the waiting chicks.*

Below: This Verreaux's eagle Aquila verreauxi *nest is clearly the product of several seasons' occupation.*

might think that the male is playing safe and making sure that she is not hungry and will not feel tempted to eat him! This may be partly true, but the main purpose of court-ship feeding is probably to give the female sufficient nutrition to build the eggs which she is soon to lay.

Many birds of prey don't bother to build nests. Almost none of the owls do – instead they take over the old nests of other birds or occupy natural hollows in trees and rocks. Some choose unusual sites. The tiny elf owl may be seen peering from holes made by other birds in the massive desert cacti of central America. The American burrowing owl can dig its own nest tunnel, but it often saves itself the effort by taking over aban-doned holes dug by gophers or prairie dogs. It is not unusual for several pairs to nest quite close together. No falcons build their own nests and neither do the vultures of the New World. Some use other birds' nests instead, but most simply lay their eggs on an open rock ledge or on the ground.

Whether or not they actually construct nests themselves, many birds of prey will use the same site again and again for years in succession. This is particularly noticeable with falcons and eagles that breed on cliffs or crags and it is quite possible that some of the favourite sites have been in use more or less continuously for hundreds of years. Because of this, an eagle's nest will often grow to be very large as the birds add more branches and twigs each time they use it. The largest one ever found was said to have been 5.4m (18ft) high and well over 1.8m (6ft) thick.

As a general rule, the smaller birds of prey lay more eggs than the larger species. Eagles and eagle owls produce only one or two eggs, falcons often lay four or five and the tiny elf owl may have a dozen in a clutch. Some raptors are able to vary the number of eggs they lay, depending on whether food is plentiful or not. As the female has to form all the eggs in her own body, she is able to produce more if she is getting plenty to eat than if food is scarce. Usually, the increase in numbers during good times is not large, although some owls can lay two or three times the usual number in times of plenty. This fact of nature means that the owls can take advantage of times when conditions are very favourable. As we saw earlier, the truly nomadic birds – like the letter-winged kite of Australia – may not attempt to breed at all when food is in very short supply. The birds that make these changes from year to year are mostly those that feed on small mam-mals, the numbers of which can rise and fall enormously from one year to the next.

Most female owls start to incubate their eggs as soon as the first one is laid. In this way, each one hatches in turn instead of all more or less at once. The chicks, therefore, are all different sizes so that, if food becomes scarce, the biggest ones take whatever their parents bring and the small ones starve. This may seem unfair but it is a way of ensuring that at least some of the young birds survive at such times. If they were all the same size and the food was divided equally between them then, in times of hardship, all of them would die.

Strangely, the same thing happens with some eagles – although they only have two chicks – and it may occur even when there is plenty of food available for both of them. Indeed the older will often attack the younger chick without any interference from the parent. Even if the younger bird is not actually killed at such an attack, it may still be ignored by the adults and allowed to starve. Nobody has yet been able to explain what possible purpose this can have – more particularly as there seems no point in the birds laying two eggs if they are not going to make at least some attempt to rear both the chicks.

When young raptors hatch, they are clad in warm, fluffy white down. At first they seem very weak and the mother bird has to coax them to eat, carefully holding out tiny slivers of meat in her beak. The bigger species must also be careful not to damage their young by treading on them and the female will curl her toes up into a ball, with the talons safely out of the way, before carefully placing her feet on each side of the chicks as she settles down to incubate them.

Throughout the period when the hen is sitting on the eggs and while the chicks are small, the male brings her food so that she does not have to leave the nest at all. Later, when the young are well developed, she may help with the hunting, but in some species the whole responsibility of finding food for the two adults and several offspring may fall to the male bird alone. When food is plentiful, a stockpile is often produced and recently killed mammals or birds are left on the edge of the nest until they are needed. This is very useful if bad weather prevents hunting for a day or two.

Usually the male plays no part in actually feeding the chicks. His duties end when he has brought the food to the nest or left it nearby for the female to collect. Male harriers usually pass the food to their mates in flight. When the hen sees the cock bird coming, she takes off to meet him; then,

Large owls, such as the milky eagle owl Bubo lacteus *(above, right) and the great horned owl* Bubo virginianus *(opposite, bottom) may have only one or two chicks, but smaller species like the screech owl* Otus asio *(opposite, top) will have more. Whether all are reared depends on how much food can be caught for them.*

Opposite, centre: A single fledgeling long-eared owl Asio otus.

Above, left: The black-shouldered kite Elanus caeruleus *is a largely nomadic species.*

when she is flying below and a little behind him, he drops his prey and she skilfully reaches out with her feet to catch it as it falls. Sometimes, a male harrier will be mated to several females all nesting in the same general area, but somehow he still finds it possible to provide them all with adequate food.

While they are small the chicks need shelter both from cold and, equally, from the hot sunshine. As they get larger, and their feathers start to grow through the down, this becomes less important and the female spends more time standing on the edge of the nest or perched on guard somewhere nearby than she does actually sheltering her young. Many birds of prey are staunch defenders of the area around the nest. Goshawks have the reputation of attacking any large creature that comes too close: one will hurtle down from the treetops to give even a bear or a wolf a savage clout and be gone again before the animal knows what hit it. Tawny owls can be extremely dangerous, and will attack the face of anybody unwise enough to interfere with their nest. Snowy owls are known to use another tactic – they draw intruders such as Arctic foxes away from the nest with a distraction display. First they flap over the ground with their wings out-

spread as if they were injured and so fool the enemy into trying to catch them. Then, when they are sufficiently far away from the area of the nest, the birds take flight and leave the confused enemy.

In the absence of their parents, older chicks are capable of making at least a pretence of ferocity should a predator approach the nest. Owlets fluff themselves out, at the same time spreading their wings and turning them forward to make themselves look as big as possible. Then they clatter their beaks noisily, as though they are just waiting for an opportunity to sink them into the enemy. Other bird of prey chicks may sit back on their tails with their wings half spread to keep their balance and their feet thrust well forward so that they can strike out with them at anything that comes within reach. Faced by an enemy much bigger than themselves, though, the chicks usually sink down into the nest and keep as still as possible in the hope that it will pass by without noticing them.

Once the young chicks are well grown, they start to exercise their wings, flapping and jumping up and down every day until finally, as much by accident as by design, the juvenile bird finds itself airborne. In this first flight, it will probably not be long before it makes a crash-landing on the ground or in a nearby tree! But from now on their progress is rapid, and they will all soon be flying well. The parents' responsibility continues, however, until the young have learned to hunt for themselves. As we have seen, hunting requires skill as well as strength and these qualities take time to develop. In some of the big eagles, the parents care for the chick until it is nearly a year old, which means that they cannot breed annually themselves. They do not need to produce lots of young if they ensure that those they do rear are given the best possible chance of reaching maturity.

For any kind of bird (or any other creature for that matter) to keep up its numbers, throughout their whole lifetime, each pair has only to produce two young that survive to breeding age. These two in turn must breed, and the species will be perpetuated. In other words, all each bird has to do is replace itself, but in fact this is not as easy as it sounds. In some species, food shortage may affect the number of eggs that the birds can lay. Chicks themselves may die because of food shortages, because they get too hot or too cold, or because they are killed by other predators. Once they leave the nest, all the young birds are exposed to a great variety of dangers and those that are unlucky or do not learn quickly enough will die. The longer the

Opposite, top: Many birds of prey, like this augur buzzard Buteo augur, *decorate the edges of the nest with fresh greenery. The reason for this, however, remains uncertain.*

At birth, chicks are covered in fine white down as seen in the augur buzzard (opposite, bottom) and Verreaux's eagle Aquila verreauxi *(right, top). Gradually quills grow through and then feathers begin to sprout from them as shown by the secretary bird* Sagittarius serpentarius *(right, bottom) and golden eagle* Aquila chrysaetos *(centre, right). As chicks grow larger, they spend less time crouched weakly in the nest and move around, exercising and flapping their wings like the ospreys* Pandion haliaetus *(centre, left).*

Opposite, centre: A chimango Milvago chimango *(a species of caracara) incubates its eggs in a nest built up to well above the water level in a South American wetland.*

adult birds are able to spend looking after their chicks, the greater their chance of reaching maturity.

Many young birds die in their first winter when food becomes scarce and competition for it is fierce. But the longer they live, the better they get at hunting and the less likely they are to fall prey to other creatures. Once they reach adulthood, there is no reason why they should not live for many years. Bigger birds of prey can reach considerable ages. In zoos, golden eagles have lived for more than forty years and eagle owls may live much longer than that. It is not likely that birds in the wild would manage to survive so long however. As soon as they get sick or injured in any way, or simply slow down with age, their chances of survival become slim.

There is no reason to feel sad at the passing of an older generation provided that there is a new one to take its place. For at least sixty million years there always has been an up and coming generation, but now the future is less certain. All over the world, wildlife is becoming less common and less varied: birds of prey, which depend on an abundance of other creatures for their own livelihood, are amongst the first to disappear. We must learn to value them for their freedom and their beauty, understand how they live, and do what we can to make sure that they survive into future ages – to float softly through the dark and soar far upon the wind.

Large raptors invest much time and effort in raising their young. Here a martial eagle Polemaetus bellicosus *(left) stands protectively at the side of its enormous nest.*

Far left: Smaller species such as the sparrowhawk Accipiter nisus *must produce more eggs and young to compensate for higher juvenile and adult mortality.*

Left, centre and bottom: Even when small and downy, all bird of prey chicks, already have the keen gaze, hooked beaks and powerful feet that they need to survive in adult life.

Acknowledgments

The publishers wish to thank the following Photographic Agencies for their help in making this book.

Ardea (London) Ltd.
Jack Bailey: 28, centre
Ian Beames: 24, bottom right; 34/35, spread, 39, bottom right
Hans & Judy Beste: 16, bottom; 28, top right; 38, inset top also title page; 39, top right; 42, top; 45 and back cover; 53, second from top
P. Blasdale: 29; 51, bottom right
R. J. C. Blewitt: 23, bottom right; 37, bottom right; 41, top right
R. M. Bloomfield: 24, left; 59, top
J. B. S. Bottomley: 7, centre right
Tom Brakefield: 40, bottom
Werner Curth: 15, bottom; 24, top; 43, top; 46
M. D. England: 23, top right; 36, top right
André Fatras: 11; 19, top right; 43, bottom; 52, main picture; 55, bottom
Kenneth Fink: 7, bottom right; 13, bottom; 14, bottom left; 15, top right; 20, top left; 21, bottom right; 24, top

right; 25, 38, bottom inset; 55, top right
R. Flemming: 6
Clem Haagner: 8, bottom left; 28, bottom; 31, bottom; 33, top; 41, centre; 56, top left
Chris Knights: 60, centre
Ake Lindau: 47, bottom
P. Morris: 9, right; 18, left; 27
Chris Mylne: 13, top and bottom; 42, bottom
Mark Newman: 55, centre
S. Roberts: 20, bottom left; 60, bottom left and bottom
Robert Smith: 7, top left
Peter Steyn: 7, top right; 10, bottom left; 20, top right; 31, top; 35, bottom right; 37, top left; 54, left; 56, top right; 59, bottom; 60, top
Jack Swedberg: 53, bottom
Alan Weaving: 30, top and bottom; 32, top; 37, bottom left; 58, bottom
Wardene Weisser: 14, bottom right; 57, centre
Tom Wightman: 8, bottom right; 36, bottom left; 53, third from top
Tom Willock: 49, bottom
also Animals Animals, RSPB